Auguries

Auguries

CLEA ROBERTS

BRICK BOOKS

LIBRARY AND ARCHIVES CANADA CATALOGUING IN PUBLICATION

Roberts, Clea, 1974–, author
Auguries / Clea Roberts.

Poems.
Issued in print and electronic formats.
ISBN 978-1-77131-451-0 (softcover).
ISBN 978-1-77131-453-4 (pdf).
ISBN 978-1-77131-452-7 (epub)

I. Title.

PS8635.O2252A95 2017   C811'.6   C2016-907493-5   C2016-907494-3

We acknowledge the Canada Council for the Arts, the Government of Canada through the Canada Book Fund, and the Ontario Arts Council for their support of our publishing program.

Canada Council   Conseil des Arts
for the Arts   du Canada

Canadian   Patrimoine
Heritage   canadien

ONTARIO ARTS COUNCIL
CONSEIL DES ARTS DE L'ONTARIO
an Ontario government agency
un organisme du gouvernement de l'Ontario

The author photo was taken by Tony Gonda.
The book is set in Novel Pro and Civita.
Cover photo © carl cash / photocase.com.
Design and layout by Natalie Olsen, Kisscut Design.
Printed and bound by Sunville Printco Inc.

BRICK BOOKS
431 Boler Road, Box 20081
London, Ontario N6K 4G6
www.brickbooks.ca

To my husband Mark
for living this life with me,
and to Linnea and Ambrose,
who will always be my best poems
and my best teachers.

Andante Grazioso

The flooded ditches
have sealed with ice.

The morning light
comes later and later —

whispering and full
of dark threads.

I've decided to speak,
to release certainty,

to take winter's ravens
as my rowdy clerics.

The street lamps bend
to the crown of frost I make
just by breathing.

If Suddenly My Dreams Are Premonitions

There is music or
there is snow falling
on the white-tailed deer.

They strip the ash berries
with precise, needful tugs.

There is music or
there is the gliding silence
between their hoofbeats
as the wind changes.

An introduction is made.
A small part of me
goes with them.

The Forest

A cold stream,
a wooden cup.

There was no question
of where you would cross
or where you
would stop to drink.

And still I ask —
what brought
you to me?

The plain succour
of my axe cleaving
the distance?

The mischief of
new brome grass
at your knees?

The trees will count
all the years we've lived,
and then they will keep
on counting,

or fall down or be
felled, or burn
standing or in a stove,

the fire a
bright prayer
releasing carbon,
all the words uttered,

our first exhale
and our last.

There will be the things
we have chosen to dwell
upon, and the things
we have chosen
to forget, as well as
the pine needles
caught in your hair,
our bodies cradled
in cacophonies
of wildflower and lichen.

But first there will be
intentions and mutability,
a study of light and clouds
through the treetops,
the subtle ways to give
ourselves completely.

The passing corvid, aware
of its reputation for intelligence,
will fly over,
clearing its throat.

February

There was darkness
until it lifted
by the strength
of its own wings.

It was quitting time.
I stumbled
from my office,
like the others that day,
blinking and tilting
toward the fresh dusk,

the indecision of light
in the ridiculous, blue sky.

Cold Snap

The simple arguments
of juncos retract
into the forest.

The house settles
in the hungry air,
its short complaints
plucking
at our sleep.

Frost climbs up
the bedroom
windows.

This is the flora
of our slumber,
the bright boughs
we breathe out
in our dreams.

The narrow light
of morning;
the wavering syllables
of the radio
indigenous to the kitchen

where you fry
bacon for our sandwiches;
the rising bread that
smells of nostalgia.

Let's be an
old couple
someday —

the visible
and the invisible
economies drifting
between us.

Maybe
they're heart
palpitations,

maybe it's
a snowplow
scraping
the chipseal road.

You are
the only audience
to my frailty.

I want to be
a winter person;

I like the way
it implies
improvement.

So cold
it squared
the truck's wheels

and unstitched
the long sleeves
of our schedules,

the sound
of distant highways
folded then placed
on the doorstep.

Tell me
how to breathe
between
the painful
and the beautiful,

my lips,
my eyelids
slow with cold.

Why She Stayed

Because she got
in on the potluck
circuit

and kept leaving
her pottery
behind.

Because the history
was like telegraph
wire — ubiquitous

and pliable —
best understood
once it tangled
into a nest.

Because her
chainsaw was bigger
than his.

Because there was
a freezer full
of moose.

Because she was
the white sheep
of the family.

Because she took
an axe to the frozen lake,
sweated hours
to cut the fishing hole

and in this way
felt the reliable deepness
of winter.

Riverine

Where the Nisutlin grew shallow
and swift, we rested our

paddles on the gunwales,
only dipping them to steer.

We watched the riverbed,
the astonishing velocity

of the round, green boulders
passing beneath us,

and the red-backed spawners

slipping upstream through
the shadows cast by clouds.

And the kingfisher
we startled into flight, gliding

furtively from one sweeper to the next,
while the small bruin raised its snout

in the air, and catching our scent,
turned back into the forest

as we drifted by
and around the bend.

Every night the wolves called
into the unreachable parts of us

and you laughed in your sleep.
It wasn't your usual laugh —

it belonged to the woman
who walked naked into the river

each morning, right to the top of her thighs,
and sunk down, purposefully,

kneeling on the soft gravel to bathe, to see
every heartache suddenly flattened

and carried away on the river's
sun-scalloped surface,

a driftwood fire
blazing on the shore.

Matins

The fridge chatters
like crickets,
which means
it's dying again.

At least this is what
you tell me as you iron
the collar of a striped shirt,
the grey steam
shushing in bursts.

It's gone on
between us like this
for years — me noticing,
you explaining, you noticing,
me explaining.

Our ghosts walk before us
into each room, adjusting the furniture,
opening the blinds.

Everything needs
translation — even for people like us,
who have eaten
from the same plate of sorrow,
pared the apple to its core.

I clear the breakfast
dishes, you wipe the table
clean of crumbs.

Your lean wrists
escape the cuffs of your sweater,
your watch five
minutes too fast.

You take your keys, your parka.
For a tall man, you
step lightly down the stairs.

I guess you are happy,
even though it's February
and we're a little crowded by
our shadows.

The new light
will breathe room
where it's needed,

the gate will swing
on its post.

As I turn off the news
I hear your tires
pull away

through the snow,
and the kettle begins
to murmur and tut.

I did not prune
the alder this year;
it traces and taps
against the house.

Now the tips
of its black branches
disclose everything
the wind knows:

topography,
the coming weather,
distance.

Whiteout, Skagway Summit

We felt dizzy and foolish,
the shadows unstitched
from our heels.

One hand on the truck's hood,
the other waving or grasping
as if to touch the blind air,
its terrifying purity
saturated with light.

Did we remember, then,
what they'd told us about
our bodies, how their
asymmetry would
lead us astray, walking slow,
unintentional circles?

Even the left lung
is smaller than the right
to make room for the heart,

its lopsided compartments
filled with different measures
of blood and desire.

Winter Sunday

It took two hours
and a mattock

to break ground
for the old dog's grave.

My lack of foresight
was a failure of sorts, but

she could have lived
another year, or at least

until the grey melt
of footsteps traced

the walk to the woodpile,
the earth sloughing its resistance.

And even with whiskey
in the coffee it took a while

to warm up — an enduring whiteness
on my knuckles where

the frost bit too hard, too long.

The Way a Winter Is Measured

If I thought badly of you,
it doesn't matter anymore;

my thin gloves and the snow
shovelling, a penance of sorts.

Sundog in the sky,
children throwing themselves

on crusted snowbanks. Inside
a message on the machine.

Tomorrow hoarfrost will settle
and the river ice will thicken.

There will be waxwings,
but the swans aren't expected

for months. And whether
I refer to calendars or mercury,

only a hard-packed path
along the clay cliffs

will measure the distance I have travelled
through my bright, ambiguous grief.

Let's talk, instead,
of forgiveness: the open arms of a sundog,

a startle of snow buntings tracing circles
in the yard, the ephemeral bloom

of flour dust in the kitchen,
the pale skin of a child's body —

how it heals itself, how it is quick with light.

Mountain Walking

These early mornings
ravens dismantle

my dreams, dropping
pine cones, then

their quivering, watery
questions, the tent

translucent as an eyelid.

Rustle of goose down, growl
of sleeping bag zipper,

sweat and woodsmoke
in Linnea's morning hair —

mountain heliotrope's slow
acquisition of the rising sun.

A slow walk
between
the krummholz
and dwarf birch.

Lichen-painted scree
to the lookout

where the soul tightens
and pulls in the wind.

Spaciously —

this is the way
the living walk

after they pierce
the firmament

with their heads.

Dust on my boots, a black
stream edged with ice,

and the whistle of the pika,
so unadorned and fierce

it tugs at the sky
where the cranes kettle

always on the verge
of an alphabet.

Letter to My Daughter

Vow

A hardscrabble climb
up the hillside,

the thin chorus
of marmots raised
by my footsteps.

Once your small brow
rests on my back,
the good weight
will hold me here

until the sun
hangs just below
the mountains,

casts light enough
to find the way home.

Aperture

No aurora tonight —
the snowflakes

admonish my eyelashes,
my cheeks,
while somewhere

the moon arcs
high over the clouds,
searching.

Degrees of Existing

You are
a pine needle
in my
teacup.

A barnacle,
a dust bunny,
a thimbleful
of decanted
light.

A minnow
swimming in
my cupped
hands.

Autumn Equinox, Second Trimester

The cries of migrating geese
trigger your kicks.

The frost bites hard;
the potato plants
flop in astonishment.

We dig buckets
of new-skinned beets,
strip the pea vines
for the chickens.

Dusk is a place
where day and night
emulsify.

Swainson's thrush,
porch light flicker.

The River

We crossed
over together,
but only I knew
it was a bridge — that there was
nothing underneath,
that it would not be there
when I looked back.

Nocturne

I'm sure
delirium
is an exotic
flower —

your
small, hard
cries,

the sky
pealing
with rain.

Naming

The real baby
and the imagined baby;

the real happiness,
the imagined happiness;
the real knowledge

and the imagined knowledge —
is one complete
without the other?

There is a common
story or grief between us;
the smell of scalp,
the smell of breast.

Will you, with your blue-black eyes,
watch the deepening
shadows, the rising light
of my face —

and see me perhaps
as I truly am,
real and imagined.

Linnaea Borealis

My hands
stroke the fine, lucid skin
of your jerky limbs.

Here's to hunger
that's bigger
than a body.
Here's to the fierce

petal of your tongue
drawing down the milk.

Berry Picking

This is how
it can begin:
You are fresh

as a new potato
tucked in my coat.
My knees stained

with cranberry,
the black spruce
creaking gently,
stirred by the wind
high above.

A love so big
I can only own
a piece of it.

My palms open
to the sky,
weighing the air —
its possibilities.

A Small Legacy

All we can give you
are the old maps,
the familiar gestures
for abundance and dearth.

We can only walk you
past fields of clover, sweeter
for being broken
by the frost, teach you

not to throw rocks at the clay cliffs
furrowed like a brow
and full of sparrows.

But here is our best advice:
nothing belongs entirely
to innocence or to blame.

Not even the moon —
it only illuminated
the place where the path

divided, or where
we turned back, or where
there was no path at all,

just the forest's worry of branches,
knitted together and waiting.

Seers

Instead of the moon,
there was a white
smudge in the sky,

snow on the river ice
blown clean enough
to be unspoken.

We built a fire
on the bank
and crouched by
its sinking light,

wiggled our toes
against the cold, and waited
for the sled dogs to pass

wild-eyed and hungry —
but only for distance.

How We Wake Somewhere Different

There is nothing lighter than the touch
that awakens. Morning brought a child

to my bedside, fingertips touching my cheek —
I did not ask for this blessing.

Is it love or bright dust
that we breathe? It will take the shape

of anything, furring it with light.

From the Restaurant at the Marina

I admire how the ocean
explains to the sky
their differences —
a cluster of sailboats
tacking in the wind,
the soliloquies of gulls,
the largesse of waves
rolling under them.

Tonight I want the special;
but before that, I want
the beautiful emptiness
of appetite, air as salty
as your shoulder blade,
the enduring melancholy
of creosote, and otters slick as midnight
running up and down the dock.

I want to perch on the rigging
of this life, smell the wind
just before it catches the sail.

Epoch

The orange, nameless cat
skulked deep in the field

divining the small panics of mice and voles
for someone else's doormat.

There were the bacchanalian cries
of coyotes, and the grey jays

shuddered from tree to tree.
If there was a moon

it didn't tell me anything
about myself, except that

my shadow was long
and humourless, that happiness

was for amateurs,
and that hunger would always rub

its head on my leg.

Spring Snowfall, Melting

Green crowns of grass
push through the snow.

Sparrows fly up before me,
their plain feathers working the air.

Against the blue sky,
they are a string of beads.

A Reliable Vehicle

It's Saturday.
If the truck
doesn't start
he'll call the neighbour
for a jump,

open hood
in the driveway.
A revelation —

it gawks all morning
at the world's
soft release.

Spring Planting

Wood ash
and bone meal —
if this is an act
of memory,
you should start
with the amendments.

The sky is a little
bleak. You feel
a grey weight
pressing behind
your eyes.

There is a root ball
in burlap, there is
a bucket of river
water tugging
at your arm.

Kinnikinnick
clipped and lifted
with your spade.

The ochre clay
slick and cold
and full of tree roots,
ligatures that snap
and pop as you
step and pry.

The blister
comes quickly —
then tears and stings
much more than
it should.

Grief is a slow
river, never freezing
to the bottom.

Grief is a good
scavenger, locates

the plangent songs
of mourning

clean and white
as gulls.

Grief is a burled log.

Cut to length, polished
and bright, it can hold
up your porch roof
for years,

greet everyone
who comes
to the door.

Grief is
spooked horses
in a storm
and you can't
find your coat.

Consider the erratic
on the lawn.
Now consider badminton
and the erratic.

Consider the lawn
at romantic lengths
and the prickly ambitions
of wild rose and caragana.

Consider clouds
of leaf-miner moths
drifting like ash, and

amidst it all
the blue spruce
just planted —

not asking
if it's better to be new
or ancient.

It doesn't matter
what you use
to dig. It doesn't matter
if it's an act of forgetting
or remembering.

The first mosquitoes
are slow and easily
persuaded by
the soft, ambivalent
gestures of your hands.

The cliff swallows
cut through
the perfect dusk
like stones on strings.

Johnson Lake, Late August

You paddle tenderly
through the chatter

of paper-thin lake ice
while I cast and troll

a line in the wake.

This is what
it's like to forgive
and yet remember.

Set a boat in the water,
push it off from shore.

Heat Wave

Water bombers
grumble in the sky.

The heat moves between us,
a slow, big-flanked animal.

And the songbirds
create a fullness
in the air,
twitches in the branches,
a twitch in the corner
of the eye.

It's a theatrical light;
it's apocalyptic.

There is a terrible,
orange sun and we are actors
with uninteresting parts:

we mow the lawns,
turn on the sprinklers,
walk the long dusty path
to the lake.

The thrushes sing
arias to dusk
and displacement.

At some point
you close the window curtains,
use a dustpan to lift
the stiff robins and waxwings
from the lawn,
feel a little guilt
and a little betrayal.

You're a person
with good intentions.
You got a job, built a house.

Everything so simple
was supposed
to be good.

Tomorrow
at the family reunion
people will sweat in the shade,
eat wilted salads
or pieces of cake
with marshmallow icing,
sigh or laugh,
rock on their heels
or sit very still
in plastic lawn chairs.

The kids will splash
in the wading pool,
their pink, sinewy legs
thin as reeds —
it would only take
feathers to make them fly.

The First Time They Saw the Whole Earth

My mother was washing dishes;
a turquoise pendant

dangled at her sternum
as she looked out onto the patio,

the bees cross-pollinating
her Mortgage Lifters,

her Big Boys, her Fourth
of Julys. My father came home

on the late bus, walked through
the dandelions with his

brown leather shoes
and fished the newspaper

from the hydrangea.
My sister chalked

a circle on the driveway
and stepped inside.

The next day, my mother
rode the gondola up the mountain

— she wanted to *really*
see the moon —

and my father discovered
country music, that he had

a voice for those sad, celestial notes.
And my sister played croquet

by her own rules, sent
balls with coloured stripes

plock plocking all over the yard.

Brother

The light from outside
the room diffused
around us like milkweed,
and everywhere
the muted buzz of electricity.

My new brother was yellow, head
shaped like a pignut, eyes darting around
like flies at a window.

I leaned over his bassinet
and touched him with one finger.

There was something in the word
I loved — brother. Someone who came
after you to latch the gate.

We Loved to Eat at Burger King

We were young; our paper crowns
nodded, our thoughts and kisses light as Styrofoam —

we hadn't yet entered the pastures of our mortality
or figured the hoof-to-square-yard ratio.

Death was a small, underpopulated town
where cats and hamsters eventually travelled,

our grief contained in the manageable handkerchief
bundles swinging behind them.

Meat was an erotic vegetable, its marbled currents
swimming on the kitchen counter, the elastic weight

slapped in the frying pan while our mothers talked
about our fathers, their indiscretions and commutes.

I remember those days as the first.
My sister stuck pussy willows up her nose (a minor

medical emergency), my brother cartwheeled
on the shag carpet through the antediluvian light,

and I fell in love with the kitchen wallpaper,
its pale yellow roses swooning in their last days of glory,

dropping petals in perpetuity on my head.

Getting Wood

It was late autumn.
They needed a freezer
full of meat, four cords
split and stacked,

to prepare themselves
for the deep nights
that would become the black,
impenetrable mornings.

At the woodlot,
the children spilled
out of the truck
with their sandwiches
and their laced boots,

watched their father
make the fierce
and elegant gestures
of the chainsaw;

its stuttering, beautiful
economy rupturing
the thin, blue afternoon.

Then they loaded
the trailer, felt the day's labour rest
on their shoulders like a pelt,

nodded at the clearing, the fine,
empty space they'd made —
the congregation of stumps.

They made it through
to spring that way, duty
sewn onto them like a
button, until the afternoons

were steeped with light,
the quixotic sound
of water dripping
from the eaves.

And, discovering
the dull carcass
of the neighbour's cat
emerging from the melting
snowbank,

realized tragedy
could be raised
to archeological
importance.

They lost their obedience.
They shucked their down vests,
left the sour, woolly air of the house
and ran for the forest.

Hunger-licked by their perfect,
feral intentions, they dispersed
like wood ash, the willow thickets
glancing and shivering behind them.

Fever Luminaria

For three nights,
the burning weight of you
draped over my body,

the smell of sweat
and dry kindling
filled up our rooms.

Everything I knew
about love
was rendered
transparent,
all my joys and sorrows
overlaid.

A blue ache of lupins;
the last sun flickering
in a vase; where my lips pressed
to your forehead
they tasted of salt.

Musica Universalis

She gives the kids
haircuts that resemble
unpredictable
weather patterns,

hangs their curls
on the rose bushes
for nesting birds.

She divides her time
between the front yard
and the backyard.

In the mornings,
she packs lunches
with fruit
from different
hemispheres,

and every evening,
she takes a pail
to the mysterious
compost

just as the air
begins to cool
and the weight of dusk
presses down
into the soil,

releasing a scent
that is more of a refrain —
sweet and drifting,
uncontainable.

Storytelling

We all fumbled for the narrative —
including you —
setting your stories

out for the last time,
reupholstering those that
would allow you to lie
more peacefully.

One night on the phone
you said, *Before I can't talk —*
think of some questions
to ask me. There might

be something I can tell you.
There might be something
you need to know.

Condolences

The tree chippers
have arrived to redact
the black boughs reaching
for the power lines;

next door, the arrhythmia
of kids on a trampoline,
their heads levitating
and chattering
above the cedar fence.

This is how you must die —
between the sounds

the world makes,
you are unmade.

Swimming

After you rose at noon,
and I curled your hair,
and you took the Pinot grigio
to steady your hands so you could
lift your breakfast spoon to your lips,

we stepped into the ocean together,
me holding your hand
like an injured bird, not out of love
but out of necessity,
the glass surface undulating
in waves up to our shoulders.

I feel so powerful, you said,
looking around, and I knew
this was how
I must have felt
when you pulled my infant
body through the water,
the two of us weightless
and in awe.

Pneumonia

Your doctor makes
a house call,

says your lungs crackle
like *footsteps*

in snow. And even though
your legs don't work
and you hate the cold,

I know you have already
thrown open the door

and are sprinting into
the dazzling whiteness
of that whole world
opening inside you.

Morning Practice

Mountain Pose

This is what the years
have written on your body:

that you are hard enough
to rise up, and soft

enough to erode.

Tree Pose

It's necessary
to sway a little
when the wind shifts.

The body nudged
off-centre
by the last swan
departing,

as the thought
of the last swan tips
into itself.

Half Moon Pose

Allow yourself
libration.

One hand
is a bright flag,

the other presses
down into a bucket
of shadow.

Find the place
where wax is stitched
to wane.

Wild Thing Pose

You're an antler just as
the velvet splits —

raked and ribboned
through pine and spruce.

A tuning fork
for the rut.

Child Pose

When we first
wore our skins,
we learned
the language
of roundness.

Rosebud.
Cloudberry.
Bead of sap.

Now
everything
is translation.

Fire Log Pose

Your hips are less
melancholy —
more butterfly.

A field mouse
curls and breathes
under each palm.

The weight of a stacked cord
and all the spaces in between.

And although
your eyes are closed,
you know the sky's intent
is cerulean.

Corpse Pose

The wind blows
clean through the willow.

The heart open, the lungs
open.

In the house of the body,
a new room much bigger
than the last.

Perseids

The wasps hung
their fine, grey lanterns
from the eaves.

All summer we dined
with them, their slow,
ravenous orbits
venerating the table,

wild notes
coming to rest
on the rim of
a water glass,
then the salmon,
then the fruit.

I've seen your hands
pour tea from a silver
thermos, consider
the cool handle of a
sharp spade,
fix light to canvas
with oil paint and brush.

I've seen your hands
fly out and flap wildly
for a moment,
then slip quietly
into your hairline or
your front pockets,
all of it ending
with a shrug or a grin.

I am sweet-blooded —
an apparition
of calamine.

You smudge the fire
with fistfuls of grass
before we unfurl
sleeping bags
in the clearing
of silver poplars.

What light remains
turns tender, apologetic.

There is a dark, quick
fluttering at the periphery:
bats arriving; or
parts of our dreams
we forgot, remembered.

The capiz
wind chimes
drift and startle —
so many
choiring moons.

A pale moth,
a kept promise,
a piece of ash
hovering then rising
from the fire,

and everywhere
meteors shooting across
the night sky,
burning out
in the atmosphere
above us, our eyes

blinking, soft,
returned
to amazement.

Acknowledgements

Thank you for support from the Yukon Government
Advanced Artist Award, the Canada Council for the Arts, the
Banff Centre for Arts and Creativity, the Yukon Foundation,
and artArctica, all of which enabled the writing of this book.

My thanks to the editors of the following publications,
where versions of some of these poems first appeared:
Arc Poetry Magazine, Contemporary Verse 2, The Cordite
Poetry Review, The Fiddlehead, The Literary Review, The New
Quarterly, Room Magazine, Make It True: Poetry from Cascadia,
and The Poet's Quest for God: 21st Century Poems of Faith, Doubt
and Wonder.

Thank you David K. MacIntyre and Carmen Braden for
composing choral arrangements based on the poems
"Cold Snap" and "Andante Grazioso."

I'd like to express my admiration and thanks to my editor,
Jan Zwicky, for her keen ear and intelligence. Also, my thanks
to Don McKay who read and commented on an earlier draft
of this book and provided such good advice. I'd like to thank
everyone at Brick Books for their support — Barry Dempster,
Kitty Lewis, and Alayna Munce. Thanks also to Natalie
Olsen of Kisscut Design.

Thank you David Stouck, Sharon Thesen, and Marjorie Dunn
for friendship, guidance, and encouragement over the years.

With warmth and esteem, "Andante Grazioso" is for Edel, and
"Riverine" is for Brandie. "Perseids" is for Don and Kate.

CLEA ROBERTS lives in Whitehorse, Yukon Territory on the Takhini River. *Auguries* is her second collection of poetry. Her debut collection of poems, *Here Is Where We Disembark* (Freehand Books, 2010), was a finalist for the League of Canadian Poets' Gerald Lampert Award for best first book of poetry in Canada, was nominated for the ReLit Award, and was translated into German (Edition Rugerup, 2013) and Japanese (Shichosha, 2017). Clea's poems have been published in journals and anthologies in Canada, Europe, the United States, and Australia. She has received fellowships from the Vermont Studio Centre, the Atlantic Center for the Arts, and the Banff Centre for Arts and Creativity and is a five-time recipient of the Yukon Government Advanced Artist Award. Clea facilitates a workshop on poetry and grief through Hospice Yukon and is the Artistic Director of the Kicksled Reading Series.